The Secrets of Secret Shopping

Mystery Shopping
Made Easy

Lynn Shelton

outskirts press

Foreword:

I'm a scheduler who has known Lynn for over ten years. She knows the mystery shopping industry backwards and forwards and has always been available for last-minute shops. I would trust any type of advice she gives you on how to be a successful mystery shopper. She has performed numerous mystery shops for different types of clients.

She has been a solid and reliable mystery shopper and is sure to have solid and reliable advice. Her book should be a go-to resource as she is a go-to mystery shopper.

You will find her book not only interesting but informative. I'm confident that this book will inspire and motivate you to be the most wonderful mystery shopper; and if you take her advice and follow through on it, you can become a solid mystery shopper too. I've been scheduling mystery shops for 21 years, and can tell you we're always looking for solid, go-to mystery shoppers in this industry and who knows, we may end up booking you for some shops someday!

We wish you the best of luck in the field. Enjoy your reading.

Dawn Hunt

Professional Mystery Shop Scheduler

"People often say seeing is believing. In this profession, receiving is believing. When the money comes it keeps coming as long as you do your part and your research. The good companies will find you to do the work!"

*Dedicated to my daughter Ingrid and my
Mother Mildred for their undying support.*

Table of Contents

CHAPTER ONE:

What is Secret Shopping?

What is it? Mystery Shopping or Secret Shopping is the ability to report accurate and detailed information. You don't show up in a funny hat and nose. The disguise has never or will ever be appropriate. The everyday Dick and Jane can do these with no problem at all. The art of Mystery Shopping originated in the "40s and 50s" as a way to reveal employees that did not represent the company satisfactorily. During the early years, Mystery Shopping was referred to as integrity shopping. Usually, in most cases the snooping was carried out by private investigators. They often posed as ordinary customers. Then when times changed and the economy became more service-oriented, more competitive larger stores saw the need for reliable feedback or intelligence about the industry. With this in mind the retail establishments turned to marketing firms, who would in turn later send the private investigator to record observations and details regarding their shopping experience.

Various businesses that deal with the public use this service. You can get paid to: have your car serviced, get a haircut, have a good meal with family or a friend, see a movie or have your pet groomed.

The compensation depends on the job you choose as a shopper, and the amount the company wishes to pay you. It may be possible to work full-time, but it is not easy. This would involve working for more than one company, or a primary company period.

The assignment types vary in price and report size:

Type	Pay	Reimbursement	Time	Report

This is available for both males and females but you are required to be at least 18 years of age. Many have full or part-time jobs--homemakers or retired persons are welcomed as well. Following directions and being very observant is a must. Dependability is one of the most sought after traits. Deadlines are involved and the company needs to be able to depend on you, the shopper.

Chapter Two:

Shopper Beware.......

Never ever, never ever pay to shop! I signed up for free and it has remained free since '05. I encourage people to visit the sites I recommend (which you will see later) that offer you the ability to sign up FREE. However, the more tests and certifications you can take and pass, the more job offers you will receive. I worked in a high-end retail store. We were shopped and many of us read the report. For this shop, our store received 5 for 5. I took it a step further and went to that company website and signed up. I was sent an assignment on the very next day. The rest is history..

(the company will be revealed in Chapter 8) I have been coasting rather smoothly ever since.

DON'T GIVE YOUR CREDIT CARD OR SEND MONEY THROUGH THE MAIL! You do not have to in order to make it in this profession. It may take you longer to get on board, but you will appreciate it in the long run. Shadowshopper.com and Sassieshop.com are very good sources to check out the business and they give you a lot of helpful tips. They also keep you aware of SCAMS. Many of the scams involve check cashing and money transfers. The reputable companies will not ask you to cash a check or send them anything. Nor will they ask you to wire or transfer funds. Just like anything else, you have to pick and choose. Some of the shops and some of the companies are not worth it, but many others are. I will not bad mouth any of the "bad apples," but I will say, proceed with caution. Like all things, there are many wolves in sheep's clothing.

Beware of schedulers that are in a hurry to get shops done. I have been the victim too many times. Schedulers, like anyone else, want to get the work off their desk. I have done a few shops that could not be scheduled, I was offered a bonus, but not paid. They claimed I did not follow directions. I did, but after they received the report, they did what they needed to do to get their fee.

Whether you are aware or not, when you sign up with the companies, you are signing as an independent contractor. They will ask for your social security number. If you are not comfortable giving this information, it may delay your pay or even the assignments you receive (if you receive any). This means you will receive a Form 1099 at the end of the year if your income exceeds $600. The company will not withhold any taxes from your pay. Be prepared to establish a PayPal account. I have had very good luck with receiving my pay through them. You will always receive a confirmation email when money is deposited into your account. Those that send checks disburse them usually one time per month. It is important to know their pay cycle, because if you miss the cut-off, it may delay your pay an additional 30 days.

FLAG: If you are asked for your bank account information or a debit card number, RUN. Turn the page. Remember, Paypal payments and paper checks are the only forms of payment. Firms that belong to MSPA are not allowed to charge its shoppers fees, so check the company credentials of those with whom you are interested in working.

Many of the companies pay between 30 and 45 days. Some go as far as 60 days. My shortest time frame for waiting has been with shopperjobs.com. They took twelve (12) days from the completion of the shops. This usually means they have the money and you completed a good report. The more questions they have to resolve, the longer it may take to receive your money. If you have time in your sched-ule, request as many shops as you like from that particular company. But as a rule of thumb, some locations are put in rotation, meaning you can only shop them every other month or maybe once a quarter. They make the rules. So be prepared to look for work often and consistently. Brush up on your negotiation skills. When you travel outside of your coverage areas, travel incentives may be available. But if you don't ask, you don't know. I have turned a $20 shop into a $35 shop because I had to drive a little. They are more prone to negotiate at the end of the month or when a deadline is close. The companies have different deadlines and guidelines they follow. Check emails daily, several times a day. And lastly, make sure they have a good contact number for you. They really do call and ask for clarifications from time to time.

Remember the scheduler will work with you. JUST ASK!

CHAPTER THREE:

Who to Work for and What to Expect

Who do you really want to work for? You have to look for the ones with the best names in the business. Check to see if they have any problems or concerns that have not been resolved. They should be MSPA certified and deemed reliable. Also, they will not ask for any upfront fees. You also want to work with companies that lay out the guidelines and what they expect from you. Their rules and procedures are consistent and do not change. If they say they want detail-oriented people, that's who they look for. Most companies have some type of questionnaire they would like for you to complete. It allows them to determine if you follow directions, read well, and understand the concepts. The instructions are explicit and they look for individuals who can be observant and can collect the data the companies have requested. This is not for everyone. Some people can't remember what they had for lunch, not to mention the color of the girl's hair and how tall she was. The best reports yield the best pay. There are bonuses involved. If the report required is too lengthy, move to the next company. You want to look for mostly yes or no questions and a brief but detailed narrative. It can be done. I do it all the time. The more you do it, the better you become.

Chapter Four:

Know Your Stuff!

Be certified. Know your stuff! The more you know, the more you are offered. The opportunities are endless in this profession. You can be everything from a shopper to a merchandiser. To be successful at evaluating you must be objective, pay attention to detail, be able to keep track of time (wear a timepiece or have one handy), remain anonymous, and lastly have a positive demeanor.

Objectivity – only use current experiences. Past visits or past employees have no bearing on the new or current report status.

Demeanor – act natural. Be cool, calm and collected at all times. The way you act determines the reaction you receive. If you are nervous, the sales associate will be nervous. It should always be business as usual, nothing extra. Drawing attention to yourself will make you memorable and that's what you don't want. It is very important to always be a "mystery".

Details – retain as much information as possible. The more you relay to the client, the more the client can accurately depict the scenario.

Timing – time allows the client to determine who was where and when. It also gives the client detailed information on lapsed time between greetings and interactions with associates.

Anonymity – letting the cat out of the bag takes the secret out of secret shopping. Shhhh!!!!!! Don't tell a single person. As long as you are natural, they will never know.

Tips for note-taking:

If you are able to shop with some type of device, take a laptop or something to record your report. Let the other person drive while you compile your information.

Use the restroom. It is a great place to jot down information.

If doing retail, take a list and reference it. You may do so in the fitting room or while walking through the store. Now that smart phones are so important, reading while walking is not uncommon. Just be careful. Text information to yourself. You blend in and look like the hundreds of others that are walking and texting. Just don't drive and text. Please be safe and pull over.

If you still carry a checkbook, make notes in the check register. This looks very natural and you don't draw any extra attention to yourself.

Since the beginning of my shopping journey, technology has really been on my side when it comes to getting the details. Camera phones, audio settings and note pads on smart phones are key features to keep you from forgetting or missing important details. Just about everyone has a cell phone. Drawing unwarranted attention is a thought of the past.

Types of Shops: Phone, Audit, Reveal, Audio, Covert

There are so many opportunities. You can actually stay at home on the phone all day and do okay. **Phone shops** range from $1.75 to $10.00. Most of the time it involves a 1-800 number for your convenience. The questions can be minimal. You can determine how many you wish to do and if it is worth your time. **Audits** range from $15 to $25 an hour. You look for information given to you by the client to see if things are being marketed properly and priced correctly. **Reveal shops** let the store know you are in there and what you are looking for. Most of the time stores want to know if managers are following the planogram for the store. Things should be in place upon your arrival. If not, the store is often penalized for not following the plan for the month or quarter.

Discreet shops involve you going in and you doing a detailed observation of the items in question. Often you are to have an interaction with one associate or more. **Audio shops** involve you wearing a wire and/or a small video device. They are used to capture exact information. This does not allow for any margin of error and the client can review the information frame by frame. In some cases, it's the shopper's word against the employees. Although this may seem invasive, many stores have video cameras but they cannot always hear without the audio being captured.

Chapter Six:

Where Your Experience Can Lead You

Knowing this business can often take you into other positions. Report editors and schedulers are often needed in various regions. They look for applicants who have worked in the business and know the business very well. That's why it is important for the report to reflect who you are and what your capabilities are. When preparing the report, you are to write it as if you are leading a blind person. The report editor should be able to picture all you are saying without question. As a demonstrator, you are allowed to interact with customers and pay attention to their comments and concerns. An interviewer is to ask questions and record the feedback. Most of these are one on one interviews. Merchandising takes place in retail establishments and may involve various duties. Some cases you take inventory of what's on the shelves and what's in stock. You are often responsible for reorders, attaching coupon displays and re-plenishing the stock. Not all tasks are done on each visit. Tasks are performed on an as-needed basis.

CHAPTER SEVEN:

People to KNOW in the Industry

The people you should know are the reputable ones. Visit www.mysteryshop.org for a list of companies that are MSPA members. This will allow you to eliminate the bad apples. Information about the validity of a mystery shopping company can be verified by visiting the website of MSPA. You can search for the company's name to verify membership and contact information. You should contact the mystery shopping companies directly. If you have trouble reaching a live person, move on to the next one. Sign up with as many companies as you can. Be patient, if you don't hear from anyone in a reasonable time, contact them. In some cases they have so much work they cannot get back to each person in a timely fashion.

CHAPTER EIGHT:

My Favorites and Why?

There are hundreds or Mystery Shopping Companies. The MSPA site has the companies listed in alphabetical order. They also have the primary contact, phone number, address and a contact email. Often, the company may be separated by region and you can contact the person in your area for information. Many of them invite the opportunity to speak with new, existing or potential shoppers. One of my all-time favorites is Lisa. When I first embarked on this journey, Lisa sent me an email and wanted to know if I was interested in helping her with a project involving cell phone stores. I scheduled a time to speak with her and we talked. She wanted to know how long I had been shopping and what I was expecting. I told her I was new but eager to learn. Lisa provided me a 30-minute tutorial over the phone and the rest really is history. I would shop 34 of the biggest cell phone retailers in North America. They all needed to be done by the same person and all within a weeks time—quite an ambitious first gig for a new shopper!

As you begin your journey, you will learn that companies will find you. Even the schedulers will contact you. Usually if you have not worked for them, they will require you to register and they will assign the shop to you. Some shops can be self-assigned, but they always state: be sure you can shop within the timeframe requested. If not, do not request the shop. The due dates associated with the shops are crucial and need to be honored.

Ones I would always recommend:

Imyst: www.imyst.com – various establishments
PO Box 7733
Ann Arbor, MI 48107
734.786.8468

Ritterassociates: www.ritterassociates.com – retail, audits
209 N. Reynolds Road
Toledo, OH 43615
419.535.5757

StrategicReflections: www.strategicreflections.com – retail,
banks
4424 Aicholtz Road
Suite C-3
Cincinnati, OH 45245
866.518.6508

ServiceEvaluations: www.serviceevaluations.com – retail,
bank, healthcare
21 Crossways Park Drive
Woodbury, NY 11797
516.576.1188

EllisProperty Management: www.epmsonline.com
– apartments
4324 N. Beltline Road
Suite C105
Irving, TX 75038
888.988.3767

Sassieshop – retail, restaurants, banks, various
www.sassieshop.com/2me
www.sassieshop.com/2dsa
www.sassieshop.com/2csi
www.sassieshop.com/2tns
www.sassieshop.com/2mysteryshoppers
(There are several others in this group as well.)

Harland Clarke: www.harland.com/mysteryshop - banks, credit unions
1100 Arizona Street
Boulder, NV 89005
800.291.6117

Second to None: www.second-to-none.com – phone shops, healthcare, foreign language shops, restaurants
3989 Research Park Dr
Ann Arbor, MI 48108
734.302.8414

Clientsmart: www.clientsmart.com – phone shops for financial institutions, Resort presentations (involves a 2-3 night stay and participating in a presentation regarding the property) – a nice vacation and you get reimbursed
1275 Shiloh Rd NW
Suite 3130
Kennesaw, GA 30144
404.388.4750

BareInternational: www.bareinternational.com – test center evaluations, fast food, customer intercept, banks, phone calls, cell phone stores, audio stores
3702 Pender Drive
Suite 305
Fairfax, VA 22030
800.296.6699
703.591.9870

Automotiveinsights: shopper.automotiveinsights.com –
automotive (inquiries on vehicles, test drives), phone calls
to dealerships, vehicle service (oil change, brakes, simple
maintenance
Two City Place Drive
Suite 200
St. Louis, MO 63141
314.812.4840

Coyle Hospitality: www.coylehospitality.com – hotel mystery shopping
244 Madison Ave #369
New York, NY 10016
212.629.2083

White Clay Consulting: whiteclay.com – financial
1515 Story Avenue
Louisville, KY 40206
502.316.6234

Person to Person: www.persontopersonquality.com – automotive, retail
2750 Prosperity Avenue
Suite 500
Fairfax, VA 22031
703.836.1517

Nsite Inc. Mystery Shopping: www.nsiteinc.com – retail
8581 Santa Monica Blvd
Suite 112
West Hollywood, CA 90069
952.451.5858
Or
4727 County Rd 101
Suite 161
Minnetonka, MN 55345

LP Innovations: www.lpinnovations.com or
www.icuassociates.com – retail
111 Speen Street
Suite 550
Framingham, MA 01701
877.574.6682 x1510

I know you are probably thinking, it has to be more companies than this. It is without a doubt. However, I have listed ones for whom I have worked successfully and ones that pay in a timely manner, representing the industry very well.

Chapter Nine:
In the End, Details and More Details

Paying attention to detail is very important. Shoppers are always given instructions on what to look for and how to make the shopping experience a typical one. Some of the primary details often requested in the report are: was the store clean, were the associates dressed appropriately and clean, number of associates working, number of customers in the store, what was around the store you visited (other stores), was the store in compliance with guidelines, time it took to be greeted or assisted. Always read the instructions. They can change at any time, up until the time the shop is conducted. Be sure you can reference a cheat sheet at all times. It helps with the little details you may forget. Review all materials and leave ahead of time if the report is time sensitive. Make sure you get a receipt. It always serves as proof that you did complete the assignment. Receipts have specific data that the client may need. Knowing and following the scenario is important too. Carefully read over the guidelines. It is good to print out the instructions and keep them with you. Determine whether or not you can pay with cash or a credit card. Some companies will only reimburse with a credit card receipt.

CHAPTER TEN:

Terms to Know - Glossary of Terms

The language is very simple. But just in case you forget, these are a few terms to always remember:

1099 – the form you will receive at the end of the year for your taxes in the event you make more than $600 with the company for which you are working.

Audio – a shop that is recorded with sound. Some states restrict these.

Clarification – a term used to let the shopper know that the information is not clear and more information may be needed.

Client – Anyone who purchases the services of another. In Mystery Shopping, the client utilizes the data for informational purposes to review policy and procedures.

Covert – a shop that is hidden or done in secret.

Customer evaluation – individuals pose as customers to evaluate customer service, selling skills, facility appearance and policy compliance.

Cybershops – Internet shopping to obtain information.

Deadline – the due date of the shop. Usually it is within 24 hours unless otherwise specified. Each company is different, so be sure you know the guidelines for due dates.

Integrity shop – shops focused on the cash transaction between the shopper and a specific employee.

Merchandising Audit – Overt/Covert to check merchandising. This includes stocking, product placement and pricing of specific items.

Mock shop – a mystery shop for which you are not paid, designed to see if you can follow directions and give detailed information.

MSPA – Mystery Shopping Providers Association. This organization will help you identify the best companies to work for and keep you informed with helpful shopping tips and meetings that will keep you abreast of the shopping industry.

MSPA Certification – Gold, Silver or Bronze – levels of certification that allow you to be placed in a pool of shoppers. Gold is the highest level. However, all companies do not honor the metals of honor.

Mystery Shopping – a shop done overtly or covertly. Information obtained is to be used to verify that associates are performing duties in compliance with company standards.

Narrative – the picture you paint with storytelling. The editors are to feel as if they are there with you during the shop. All details should be crystal clear.

 Operations audit – Overt/Covert evaluations regarding operational guidelines. Based on actual policy compliance.

Overt – a shop that is visible, done in the public and can be observed.

Paypal – an account this is set up in order to receive shopper payments. Although paper checks are still issued, many companies ask that you have and maintain a PayPal account.

Price audit – making store visits and verifying price points for the client to determine if prices are comparable to the competitor and to see if the prices are up to date.

Reimbursement – the amount paid for an item purchased. Sometimes there is a minimum required to get your fee and reimbursement (read all the fine print)..

Report editor – the person responsible for relaying the detailed information to the client. The narrative should be written as if they were there personally.

Revealed shop – a shop when you announce that you will be conducting an audit. You are usually directed to store management to inform them of the shop.

Scheduler – the person with whom you want to have a great relationship. The scheduler is responsible for sending out the request for work and booking the shopper. Always keep an open line of communication and if something changes, notify your scheduler immediately. Reschedules are offered with proper notice. They are easy to work with, but request you are cognizant of their time and authority.

Shadowshopper – website containing information on types of shops, certifications, various guidelines, and helpful information. There are also certification tests you can take on this site which will allow you to be more marketable. Please note that after tests are taken, shops need to be done to show that you are qualified. Having the certification does not mean you can carry out the shop effectively.

Shop fee – the amount paid for the shop.

Telephone shops – conducted over the phone to obtain information regarding a product or service.

Video – a shop that is recorded with pictures. Some states restrict these.

Just a few things to remember:

1. There is always work.

2. Obtain as much training as possible.

3. Brush up on your writing skills.

4. Be on time.

5. Never reveal yourself, unless it is a reveal shop.

6. Understand that if you don't follow guidelines, you may not be compensated for your work.

7. Try to develop a good rapport with a few schedulers.

8. Sometimes you interview as if it's a 9-5.

9. Be prepared to complete a 1099.

10. Have a valid social security number

11. Be honest about your background, some require background checks.

12. Have valid driver's license

13. Have current vehicle insurance.

14. Be able to transmit information in various forms – fax, email, scan, upload.

15. Maintain an open line of communication with the company you represent.

16. If you are asked a specific question, be open and honest.

17. Never take family/friends unless it is required/allowed in the shopper instructions.

18. Never provide information if you did not do the work yourself.

19. Don't draw attention to yourself.

20. Most important, try to attend at least one Mystery Shoppers conference; you will be glad you did. They take place a few times per year: https://mspa-americas.org/events

Businesses/Brands I have performed services:

All State
State Farm
Geico
AARP
United Health Care
Cadillac
Ford
Chevrolet
Mercedes Benz
BMW
Nissan
Merrill Lynch
Bank of America
PNC Bank
FNCB
Lego
Zales
Tommy Hilfiger
Coach
Bose
Verizon
Sprint
AT&T
Xfinity/Comcast
Spectrum
Papa John's

Jiffy Lube
Amazon
Seasons 52
Texas Roadhouse
Yankee Candle
Party City
Aveda
Bed Bath & Beyond
Ross's
REI
Off Fifth
Coach
Louis Vuitton
Apple
Regus
Rodizio Grill
Southwest Airlines
Hilton

As this all comes to a close, I would like to thank the following:

I thank God for putting the right people in the right place at the right time…………………….there have been many.

My family, past and present:
Mildred Crawford Shelton – 12/6/1942 – 10/4/2016
Charles Marvin Shelton – 2/10/1932 – 9/14/2011
Ronald Shelton – 11/6/1972 – 8/3/2018
Ingrid Dan'Yelle – you always believe I can ☺

RSG – they gave me my first big gig! Thanks LVK..

All of the companies I have and continue to work for, I appreciate you all.

NCJUA and Alternative Claims for the financial stability to get this done.

My LinkedIn connection…Justin Key – he told me to go for it…I did it